B53 087 978 9

D0491392

KNOW IT ALL

BIG MACHINES

Andrew Langley

W

FRANKLIN WATTS

LONDON • SYDNEY

Franklin Watts
338 Euston Road
London NW1 3BH

Franklin Watts Australia
Level 17/207 Kent Street
Sydney, NSW 2000

This edition © Franklin Watts 2014

All rights reserved.

Series editor: Amy Stephenson
Planning and production by Discovery Books Ltd
Editor: James Nixon
Series designer: D.R. ink
Picture researcher: James Nixon

Picture credits: cover image (kaband/Shutterstock)
AGCO Corporation: p. 8 top and bottom (Challenger). Alamy: pp. 23 (EuroStyle Graphics), 24 top (William Caram). Corbis: pp. 7 (Charles W Luzier?Reuters), 13 bottom (Patrick Pleul/EPA). Defence Images: p. 29 top (© Crown Copyright/MOD, Image from www.photos.mod.uk, Reproduced with the permission of the Controller of Her Majesty's Stationery Office). Foto Flite: p. 24 bottom. Getty Images: 6 bottom (Lester Lefkowitz), pp. 11 bottom (Lester Lefkowitz), 13 top (Lester Lefkowitz), 17 (Johan Nilsson/AFP), 18 left (narvikk), 20 (David McNew), 21 top (Bloomberg), 21 bottom (Johannes Simon), 25 top (Bernd Otten/AFP). Rex Images: p. 28. Shutterstock: pp. 2 and 22 bottom (vadimmmus), 4 (Mik Lav), 5 top (dedi57), 6 top (MARCELODLT), 9 (Neale Cousland), 10 (Stanislav Komogorov), 12 (Stasis Photo), 14 top (T-Design), 15 top (James Steidl), 15 bottom (kekyalyaynen), 16 top (Chris Hellyar), 16 bottom (kaband), 18 top-right and middle-right (James Jones Jr), 19 (Mark Hall), 22 top (Andrey Degtyaryov), 26 (Andrey Yurlov). Terex Corporation: p. 11 top. Wikimedia: pp. 5 bottom (Wendy Mann), 14 bottom (Haakman), 25 bottom (LTJG Chuck Bell/US Navy), 27 top (RFM57), 27 Bottom (David Gubler), 29 bottom (Sierra Nevada Space Systems).

Every attempt has been made to clear copyright. Should there be any inadvertent omission please apply to the publisher for rectification.

Dewey number: 621.8
ISBN: 978 1 4451 3593 9

A CIP catalogue record for this book is available from the British Library
Printed in China

Franklin Watts is a division of Hachette Children's Books,
an Hachette UK company.
www.hachette.co.uk

CONTENTS

MONSTER MACHINES   4

TRUCKS   6

TRACTORS AND ROAD TRAINS   8

DIGGERS   10

MASSIVE MINERS   12

CRANES   14

BULLDOZERS   16

DRILLING MACHINES   18

TUNNELLING MACHINES   20

PLANES   22

SHIPS   24

TRAINS   26

MONSTERS OF THE FUTURE   28

QUIZ   30

GLOSSARY   31

WANT TO KNOW MORE?/INDEX   32

All words in **bold** can be found in the glossary on page 31.

MONSTER MACHINES

What's the biggest machine you've ever seen? A bus? A helicopter? A yacht? All of these are big – but they can look tiny in comparison with the real giants. Monster trucks, massive cranes, diggers and oil tankers are some of the largest machines ever made.

GIANT TASKS

Why do they need to be so huge? Because each of them has a special job to do, which smaller machines can't do. Some are designed to lift or carry massive loads. Some take vast bites out of the earth, to dig up **minerals** or re-shape the land. Others drill their way through mountains or under the oceans.

AMAZING FACT
Biggest ever?

The Large Hadron Collider (LHC) near Geneva in Switzerland is probably the biggest machine ever built. It fills a circular tunnel measuring 27 kilometres all the way round, which crosses the border into France. Over 10,000 scientists were involved in designing it. The LHC fires **particles** at huge speeds around the tunnel, as part of a science research programme to explore the basic building blocks of the universe.

This giant digging machine uses buckets on a huge spinning wheel to strip away layers of the earth.

TAKING CONTROL

All of these giant machines still need humans to operate them. Big machines such as cranes or **excavators** have many different controls. Oil tankers (above) and cargo planes have even more complex systems. Operators must have very special training to take charge of them.

TRUE OR FALSE?

One of the biggest modern machines is a spider. **True or False?**

TRUE! The mechanical spider *La Princesse* is a piece of art built in France in 2008. It weighs 37 tonnes and is as tall as a house. Operated by up to 12 people, it walks at 2 mph (3.2 kph) and can set off huge water cannons, flames and hundreds of fireworks.

TRUCKS

Trucks are huge, strong vehicles used for carrying heavy loads, such as factory goods or large amounts of rock from **quarries**. Some trucks are real giants. They are so big that they can't travel on ordinary roads. They work in mines and quarries and on construction sites – and many other unusual places.

Giant mining trucks can transport vast amounts of rock.

MINING MONSTERS

Mining trucks (above) are the biggest and strongest trucks in the world. These mammoth machines are built specially for mining work, and can carry up to 400 tonnes of soil and rock at a top speed of 40 mph (64 kph). A mining truck is a **dump truck** with a bed that can be lifted at one end to unload the contents.

Dump trucks like these are as high and wide as a house. They have enormous wheels and tyres that are taller than two people. They need these to carry their massive loads over rough ground.

TRUE OR FALSE?

Roads have to be closed to other traffic when a giant dump truck moves to a new site. **True or False?**

FALSE! The truck is taken to pieces and the parts are delivered separately. Then the truck is reassembled at the site.

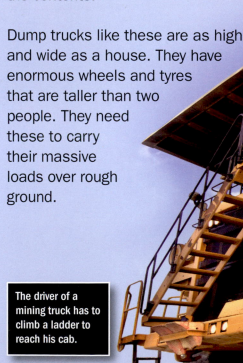

The driver of a mining truck has to climb a ladder to reach his cab.

AMAZING FACT
World's slowest space shuttle

A gigantic rocket blasts off from the launch pad and roars into the sky. It is carrying an enormous shuttle into space at incredible speed. But on the ground these spacecraft move very slowly. They are carried to a launch pad on vast crawler-transporter trucks (right), which move at just 1 mph (1.6 kph)!

A gigantic crawler-transporter truck takes up the whole road as it carries a space shuttle to its launch pad.

TRACTORS AND ROAD TRAINS

The most powerful tractors have eight wheels and massive engines.

A tractor is a powerful vehicle made to haul heavy **trailers** and machinery. The bigger the trailer, the bigger and stronger the tractor has to be.

TRACTORS ON THE FARM

Farm tractors are a familiar sight, pulling ploughs or trailers. Some of them are huge, and have four sets of large, separately powered wheels. The biggest farm tractor of all is the US Williams *Big Bud*. This monster weighs over 45 tonnes and can plough up to eight hectares of land an hour.

Some modern tractors don't have wheels at all. Instead, they run on **crawler tracks** like army tanks, which allow them to move more easily over rough or muddy fields. These tracks are made of rubber and **reinforced** with steel.

TRACTOR JOKE

Q Why did the farmer sleep under his tractor?

A Because he wanted to get up oily!

Crawler tracks stop large tractors from sinking into soft, muddy ground.

A truck that can have large trailers attached to its back is sometimes called a tractor unit.

ROAD TRAINS

Trucks that haul trailers on roads are another kind of tractor. Some are powerful enough to pull two or more trailers. These combinations are known as road trains. They are used to carry huge amounts of **freight** over long distances in remote and uncrowded areas of Australia, Argentina and the USA.

RECORD BREAKER

The longest road train ever, stretched for over a mile – 1,474 metres! It consisted of 112 trailers pulled by a single Mack Titan tractor. To break the world record, the train travelled 100 metres along a public road in Queensland, Australia, in 2006.

DIGGERS

A digger's arm reaches forward and lunges down towards the earth. The bucket claws into the ground, scooping out a huge lump of soil and rock. The cab of the digger swivels and then the bucket tips its load to one side. Big diggers can move hundreds of tonnes of **rubble** in one day. They can be used for many other construction jobs as well, from knocking down buildings to digging trenches and laying roads.

PARTS OF A DIGGER

- The platform is the main body of the digger. Inside it is the engine and fuel tank.
- The undercarriage is beneath the platform. This contains the tracks or wheels which move the digger along.
- The cab where the operator sits is set on top of the platform. Most digger cabs can swivel around in a complete circle.
- The arm is connected to the platform. It is made of two parts – the boom and the dipper arm. A bucket is attached to the end of the arm.

Dipper arm

Boom

Bucket

Arm

Cab

Platform

Tracks

Cylinder

Ram

AMAZING FACT
The biggest digger

The Caterpillar 6090FS (right) is the biggest shovel-digger in the world. It is so massive that it has to be powered by two engines. The digger can scoop up to 9,900 tonnes of material an hour. You could buy one for just £6.8 million ($11 million)!

HYDRAULICS

The arms and buckets of diggers are moved by oil under pressure. Rods, called rams, are attached to the arms. The rams are fitted inside **cylinders**. When the digger's engine pumps oil into or out of the cylinder, the rams move up or down – and so does the arm. This is called **hydraulic** power. The driver uses levers in the cab to operate the hydraulic system and control the boom, dipper arm and bucket.

WHEEL LOADERS

A wheel loader is an earthmover on wheels. It uses its extra-large bucket to scrape up material from the ground and load it into a truck. Some wheel loader buckets are enormous. The Le Tourneau L2350 has a bucket so big you could fit a fire truck inside!

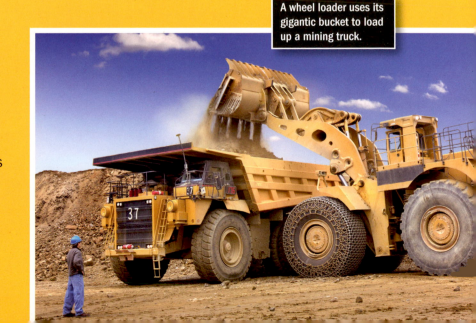

A wheel loader uses its gigantic bucket to load up a mining truck.

MASSIVE MINERS

Imagine an excavator so big it needs a crew of five to operate it. It is as long as two football pitches, and as high as the top of a stadium. It is so powerful that in a single day it can dig up an area the size of yet another football pitch – but 20 metres deep! And it weighs an amazing 14,000 tonnes.

BUCKETS ON WHEELS

This is the Bagger 288, a bucket-wheel excavator, and one of the largest land vehicles ever built. Bucket-wheel excavators (below) are used in **open-cast mines**. They lumber very slowly across the landscape, digging up minerals from the surface of the Earth faster than any other machine.

A bucket-wheel excavator has a gigantic wheel on a long boom at the front. Fixed around the outside of the wheel are as many as twenty buckets. As the wheel spins round, the buckets cut into the rock surface and scoop up coal. A series of **conveyor belts** carry the rock down the boom and through the body of the machine, loading it into trucks at the rear.

A bucket-wheel excavator scoops up material as the wheel turns.

DRAGLINE EXCAVATORS

A dragline excavator has a massive boom at the front, which can be as long as 100 metres. From this boom, a huge bucket swings out forward on the end of a cable. The bucket lands on the ground and is then dragged back by the cable. It scoops up its load from the surface of the Earth.

TRUE OR FALSE?

Dragline excavators can cause power **blackouts**. True or False?

TRUE! Some draglines need so much power than they can't run on normal fuel. They run on electricity instead. Sometimes, they take such a huge charge from the power grid that it shuts down – causing a blackout.

AMAZING FACT
Biggest of all

The largest mobile land machine of all is not a digger but a bridge (right)! The F60 Overburden Conveyor Bridge uses wagons on rails to shift millions of tonnes of waste soil, collected by bucket-wheel excavators from mines in Germany. It is 80 metres high and over 500 metres long.

Huge cranes are used to build and unload ships.

CRANES

Cranes tower over our cities. Their structures look dangerously spindly and fragile, yet they are immensely strong, lifting the parts to construct super-tall buildings. Other massive cranes load and unload cargoes in dockyards. Cranes also have a vital role in the construction of ships, and they move heavy materials in factories. Huge cranes on ships are used to recover wrecked vessels from the seabed.

TOWER CRANES

Tower cranes are often the tallest machines you can see. They raise steel **joists**, aluminium sheets and other items from the ground to the tops of new skyscrapers, so they can be fitted into place. The highest tower cranes are nearly 125 metres high.

AMAZING FACT
Champion weightlifter

The Taisun shipyard crane in Yantai, China, is the most powerful crane in history. Its job is to help build oil rig platforms. In 2008, the Taisun set a new world record for lifting the heaviest weight – a staggering 20,133 tonnes.

The Taisun crane holds up the deck of an oil rig weighing over 17,000 tonnes.

PARTS OF A TOWER CRANE

- The mast is attached to a concrete base.
- The slewing unit on top of the mast contains the crane's motor.
- The long jib is the part that does the lifting.
- The counter-jib holds a counterweight, which stops the crane falling over.
- The crane operator sits in the cab.

OVERHEAD CRANE

An overhead crane pours a heavy container of liquid metal.

Counter-jib

Jib

Cab

Counterweight

Slewing unit

Mast

Overhead cranes can move sideways along a horizontal beam. They are used in factories, for shifting heavy loads. But their most important job is in steel **foundries**. Besides moving **raw materials** and finished products, overhead cranes lift and pour enormous containers of molten (melted) steel. These containers can hold over 300 tonnes of liquid metal, heated to around 1,700°C.

BULLDOZERS

Do you want to clear and flatten a site ready for building? Then you need a bulldozer. It has a giant metal blade, which pushes huge amounts of rock, soil and other waste into heaps. Bulldozers are used on construction sites and at quarries and factories. **Armoured** bulldozers are even used on battlefields to clear away obstacles.

BULLDOZER JOKE

Q What do you call a bull when it's asleep?

A A bull-dozer! (Actually you can call it anything you like, because it's asleep!)

Ripper

PARTS OF A BULLDOZER

The bulldozer runs on a pair of tracks. These are often very wide, and have ridges, which help the machine grip on muddy or rough ground. Above them is the body that contains the cab and the engine.

A bulldozer's blade is mounted at the front. The blade can be set straight, or at an angle so that material will be pushed to one side. At the back of the bulldozer is the ripper. This is a long metal claw for loosening hard ground or rocks.

Blade

Cab

Tracks

A snow plough uses a huge blade at the front and rotating brushes towards the back to clear the snow from an airport runway.

SNOW MOVERS

A snow plough is a kind of bulldozer that scrapes snow and ice off roads. The biggest are used at airports to keep runways clear (above). These have huge blades as big as 8 metres wide, large rotating brushes and high-speed fans to blow away the snow. These snow movers can clear a huge runway in about 30 minutes. Snow plough blades can also be fitted to the front of trains to scrape snow from railway tracks. In some US cities, they are fitted to the front of rubbish trucks too.

AMAZING FACT
Superdozer!

The monster among bulldozers is the Japanese Komatsu D575A-3SD. Its blade is 8 metres wide and over 3 metres high. The Komatsu is so powerful that if you set it to drive in a straight line, it would probably carry on through buildings and forests until it ran out of fuel.

TRUE OR FALSE?

The word 'bulldoze' comes from a Greek word meaning 'to push rocks'. **True or False?**

FALSE! 'Bulldoze' comes from an American term 'bull dose'. This was the name for a drug powerful enough to put a bull to sleep. It came to mean something so strong that it could push aside any obstacle.

DRILLING MACHINES

A lot of valuable and important materials lie deep under the ground. Machines with massive drills (left) **bore** down into the Earth to locate fuels such as oil and gas. Marine drills bore into the seabed, far below the ocean's surface. Other drills go in search of something even more important – water.

Drill bit

Casing

GOING DOWN

The drill hangs from a very tall structure called a drilling derrick. At the end of the drill is the **drill bit**. This is made of diamond, or of a very hard metal called **tungsten-carbide** steel. It cuts down into the Earth, making a hole nearly a metre wide. As each section is drilled, a pipe called a casing is lowered into the hole to stop the sides collapsing.

The drill bit spins very fast, creates a lot of **friction** and gets very hot. A liquid, usually made of mud and oil, is pumped down the casing to cool the drill bit. The fluid is pumped back to the surface, and brings with it the waste bits of rock and soil cut by the drill.

After a drilling machine has drilled and lined a hole, the oil, gas, water or other materials can be brought to the surface.

OIL PLATFORMS

Drilling for oil at sea is a difficult and dangerous task. There are two main types of drilling platform. Where the sea is shallow enough, fixed platforms stand on the seabed on concrete or steel legs. In deep seas, floating 'spar' platforms are moored to the seabed with cables. They have heavy counterweights fixed underneath to keep them upright.

AMAZING FACT

The deepest hole

In August 2012, oil workers drilled the world's deepest hole off the island of Sakhalin in Russia. The drill reached down over 12,000 metres into the Earth's **crust**!

BIG MACHINES JOKE

Q Why did the tunneller quit his job?

A It was boring!

A tunnel-boring machine breaks through the other side of a mountain after digging a four mile (6.5 km) tunnel.

TUNNELLING MACHINES

A massive head chomps slowly through the mountain. It moves forward slowly, spinning so that its teeth eat away at the rock. This is a tunnel-boring machine (TBM) at work. Machines like this bore new tunnels deep underground for roads and railways. They can dig through anything from rock to soft sand.

TRUE OR FALSE?

The Channel Tunnel between Britain and France took nearly 200 years to dig. **True or False?**

TRUE! – sort of! The very first plan for a Channel Tunnel was drawn up in 1802, but nobody took it seriously. Work on the modern tunnel only began in 1988. It was completed in 1994.

INTO THE DARK

A TBM is a tube shape, standing as high as 20 metres. At the front is the head, which does the cutting. The cut material goes in through the head, and is taken away by a conveyor belt. The strong tube acts as a shield, which stops the tunnel from collapsing. The machine also strengthens the tunnel walls by installing concrete sections as it moves forward.

AMAZING FACT

The first tunnelling machine

The tunnelling shield was invented by Marc Brunel in 1825. He used it to dig a tunnel beneath the River Thames in London. The shield was simply a moving frame, on which miners hacked away rock and mud with axes called picks. The tunnel took 18 years to finish.

Head

UNDER MOUNTAINS AND CITIES

At this moment, giant TBMs are cutting the world's longest tunnel, under the Swiss Alps. When the tunnel is finished in 2018, it will stretch for 38 miles (57 km). Other machines are working deep under New York City. They are digging out tunnels for new railway lines.

Work has begun on the world's longest tunnel, deep beneath the Alps. When it is finished the tunnel will be used by high-speed trains.

PLANES

Have you watched a plane high up in the sky on a clear day? It looks tiny and slow-moving, but in fact it is enormous, and moving very fast. Modern passenger aircraft are at least 70 metres long. They cruise at more than 500 mph (800 kph), and fly over 7 miles (11 km) above the Earth's surface – well above clouds and bad weather.

GIANTS OF THE SKIES

Aircraft just keep getting bigger. The Airbus A380 is the biggest passenger airliner in the world. It has a wide body, two passenger decks, and can carry over 800 passengers. The fuselage (body) is built of aluminium, and other parts are made of plastics reinforced with **carbon fibre**. These are light, but very strong and flexible.

Airbus A380

AN225 Cossack

The biggest aircraft of all today is the Russian AN225 Cossack. It carries cargo, and is so heavy that it needs six engines to fly. The Cossack has a giant **wingspan** of 88 metres – almost the same length as a football pitch.

INTO THE AIR

How does a big, heavy airliner get off the ground? The answer is in the wings, which are curved on top and flatter below. As the plane moves forward, air flows over both sides of the wing. But it flows faster over the top, because it has further to go. This lowers the **air pressure** on the top, while the pressure on the bottom stays the same. The difference in pressure creates 'lift', which allows the moving plane to climb into the sky.

TRUE OR FALSE?

The world speed record for a cardboard aircraft is 100 mph. **True or False?**

TRUE! A plane made of cardboard flew that fast over the Arizona desert in 2012. It was 14 metres long and had no engine or pilot. It was pulled into the sky by a helicopter.

The *Spruce Goose* has the largest wingspan of any aircraft in history.

AMAZING FACT
Spruce Goose

The widest aircraft ever was built in the USA in 1947. Called *Spruce Goose*, it was as tall as three houses and its body was made of wood. It had a wingspan of 97 metres, which gave it room for eight engines. *Spruce Goose* was a flying boat which meant it could take off and land on water. But this monster plane made just one flight – which lasted one minute. It was too big and unstable to develop further, and it is now in a museum.

SHIPS

Ships do things no other machines can do. They can carry much bigger cargoes than trucks or trains. And they can make even longer journeys than planes. Ships can also be used for massive jobs such as breaking paths through sea-ice or **dredging** mud from harbours and rivers.

A supertanker sits in a harbour during the final stages of its construction.

SUPERTANKERS AND CONTAINER SHIPS

Ships are the largest long-distance machines in the world. The real giants are the supertankers, which carry oil across the oceans. The biggest of these was the *Seawise Giant*, which was 450 metres long. When sailing at top speed, it needed a staggering 5.5 miles (8.9 km) to come to a stop.

AMAZING FACT
The floating vacuum cleaner

The Dutch ship *Queen of the Netherlands* (right) is a **suction** dredger which clears channels deep enough for big ships to use. It trails a long pipe down into the water to suck up silt, sand and mud from the seabed, like an enormous vacuum cleaner. The head of the pipe is a massive six metres wide. The vessel has also been used to recover parts from aircraft that have crashed into the sea.

The *Emma Maersk*, is one of eight E class container ships currently in use.

Some of the biggest working ships are the E class, such as the *Emma Maersk* (above). Built in Denmark, the *Emma Maersk* transports cargo in large metal containers all over the world. She can carry over 14,000 of these containers. Even bigger are the Triple E class container ships.

SHIPLIFTERS!

A heavy-lift ship is so strong that it can raise other big ships out of the water. It is used to carry damaged ships to a safe place for repair. A heavy-lift ship can partly **submerge** itself by filling special tanks with water. The damaged ship can then be floated into position above the heavy-lift ship. When the heavy-lift ship pumps the water out of its tanks its deck rises back up, lifting the damaged ship safely on board. Even large warships can be lifted and transported in this way.

SHIP JOKE

Q Which part of a ship is made out of cards?

A The deck!

The US Navy uses a heavy-lift ship called *Blue Marlin* to carry damaged warships back to the United States.

MONSTERS OF THE FUTURE

What kinds of mega-machines will be built in years to come? At this moment, scientists and engineers are at work on many amazing new designs. Here are a few of them.

BIGGER DIGGERS

The next generation of excavators will be larger, safer and more powerful. Hydraulic systems will be replaced by small individual motors for each of the moving parts, powered by **fuel cells**. For really dangerous work, the cab can be removed, and the driver can operate the digger from a safe location nearby.

TRUE OR FALSE?

Only old-fashioned ships have sails. **True or False?**

FALSE! Many big cargo ships are now being designed to use the power of the wind. Besides their engines, they will have ranks of sails at least 50 metres high. The sails will automatically fold themselves up in rough weather or when the ship is in dock.

TRUCKS

Long-distance cargo trucks will look very different in the future. Their bodies will be **aerodynamically** shaped, and their wheels will be set wider apart so they grip the road better. This will help the vehicle to accelerate more quickly, but use less fuel.

This truck of the future has been designed with an aerodynamic shape so that it can travel faster.

Aircraft of the future may simply look like one giant wing.

PLANES

Future aircraft will have surprising shapes. One idea is the 'flying wing', which is simply one giant wing with the cabin space inside. Some new planes will use different kinds of fuel, such as **hydrogen**, instead of fossil fuels such as **kerosene**. At the same time, planes will become faster. A new engine called a 'scramjet' is being developed, which will push aircraft to speeds of over ten times the speed of sound!

AMAZING FACT

A new era of spacecraft

The **space shuttle** made its last flight in 2011. It could be replaced by the *Dream Chaser*. This new spacecraft will ferry people and goods to the **International Space Station** (ISS), 1,200 miles (2,000 km) away from Earth. One of the aims of the *Dream Chaser* project is to take tourists on trips into space and to the ISS. It is planned to start operations in 2016.

The *Dream Chaser* is designed to carry up to seven people into space.

QUIZ

How much have you learned from reading this book? Here is a quiz to test your memory.

1. What kind of machine was the giant *Big Boy*?
2. What holds the counterweight which keeps a tower crane upright?
3. In which country is the world's deepest hole?
4. What kind of excavator is the Bagger 288?
5. What is the record number of trailers pulled by a road train tractor?
6. What type of power system is used to move the bucket of a digger?
7. What is a bulldozer's ripper used for?
8. How is a 'spar' oil platform fixed in place?
9. What type of crane is used to pour molten metal in steel foundries?
10. In which two countries is the Large Hadron Collider?
11. What is the biggest passenger plane in the world?
12. What kind of cargo is carried by supertankers?
13. What's the top speed of a crawler transporter carrying a space shuttle?
14. What is a suction dredger mainly used for?
15. Which part of a digger's arm is nearest to the driver?

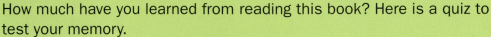

AMAZING FACT
How many elephants?

1 African elephant	weighs 5 tonnes
Tractor	weighs the same as 9 elephants
Bulldozer	= 30 elephants
Cargo plane	= 57 elephants
Mining truck	= 125 elephants
Digger	= 196 elephants
Bucket-wheel excavator	= 2,800 elephants
Supertanker	= 18,000 elephants

GLOSSARY

aerodynamic made with rounded or smooth edges and outlines to reduce wind resistance

air pressure the force of air pressing down on an object

armoured protected with a tough metal layer

blackout when the electricity supply fails in part of a country

bore to make a hole with a drill

carbon fibre an extremely strong and light material in which several thousand fibres of carbon are bonded together in crystals

conveyor belt a rubber and steel belt on rollers that carries material from one place to another

crawler track a steel band passing round the wheels of a vehicle for travel on rough ground

crust the top layer of rock on planet Earth

cylinder a tube-shaped container that holds liquid under pressure

dredge to scoop up objects and mud from a river or seabed

drill bit the cutting part at the tip of the drill

dump truck a truck with a body that tilts at the back for unloading

efficient working without too much effort or cost

excavator a machine that digs out soil and rock from the ground

foundry a factory where raw materials are converted into metals, such as iron and steel

freight goods transported in bulk by trucks, trains and ships

friction the rubbing of one surface against another

fuel cell a power system which uses hydrogen instead of a fossil fuel, such as coal or oil

hydraulic relating to power that comes from pushing liquid through a tight space

hydrogen a colourless gas

International Space Station a structure where scientists do research in space, placed in orbit around the Earth in 1998

joist a beam supporting parts of a building

kerosene a thin oil used as a fuel for jet aircraft

locomotive a railway vehicle with the power to pull freight wagons or passenger carriages

mineral natural substances that are mined from under the Earth's surface

open-cast mining a system of removing valuable materials from the surface of the earth by digging open pits instead of tunnels

particle one of the very small pieces that makes up everything in the universe

quarry a place where stone or other materials are extracted from the Earth

raw material basic material from which a product is made

reinforced given added strength

rubble pieces of rock, mud and other waste material

space shuttle the reusable space craft used for missions into space between 1981 and 2011

submerge go below the surface of the water

suction the removal – or sucking out – of air, to force fluid into an empty space

trailer an unpowered vehicle towed by another

tungsten carbide an extremely hard, fine grey powder, produced by heating the metal tungsten and the chemical element carbon to a very high temperature

wingspan the distance between the tips of the two wings of an aircraft

WANT TO KNOW MORE?

Here are some places where you can find out a lot more about big machines:

WEBSITES

http://www.youtube.com/watch?v=97mFpyjT7ck
Link to videos of giant dumpers and diggers in action.

http://www.bukisa.com/articles/40463_worlds-largest-machines-ever-built
More on the top monster machines.

BOOKS

Record Busters: Machines, Clive Gifford, (Wayland, 2014)

Inside Giant Machines (Explore Your World), Steve Parker, (Miles Kelly 2012)

The Wold in Infographics: Machines and Vehicles, Jon Richards and Ed Simkins, (Wayland, 2014)

The World's Biggest Machines (Extreme Machines), Marcie Aboff, (Raintree 2011)

Website disclaimer:
Note to parents and teachers: Every effort has been made by the Publishers to ensure that these websites are suitable for children, that they are of the highest educational value, and that they contain no inappropriate or offensive material. However, because of the nature of the Internet, it is impossible to guarantee that the contents of these sites will not be altered. We strongly advise that Internet access is supervised by a responsible adult.

INDEX

Airbus A380 21

Big Boy 27
buckets 4, 10, 11, 12, 13
bucket-wheel excavators 4, 12, 13
bulldozers 16–17

cabs 6, 10, 11, 15, 16, 26, 28
cargo 5, 14, 22, 24, 25, 27, 28
container ships 24, 25
cranes 4, 5, 14–15
crawler tracks 7, 8, 10, 16

diggers 4, 10–11, 28
dragline excavators 13
dredgers 24
drills 18–19
dump trucks 6

electricity 13, 26, 27
engines 8, 10, 11, 16, 23, 26, 27, 28, 29
excavators 5, 12, 13, 28

factories 14, 15, 16
fuels 13, 17, 19, 26, 28, 29

heavy-lift ships 25
hydraulics 11, 28

Large Hadron Collider (LHC) 4
locomotives 26, 27

mines 6, 12, 13
mining trucks 6, 11
motors 15, 26, 28

oil 11, 18, 19, 24
oil rigs 14, 19
oil tankers 4, 5, 24

planes 5, 22–23, 29

quarries 6, 16

rams 11
road trains 9
roads 6, 7, 9, 10, 17, 20, 26, 27, 28

ships 14, 24–25, 28
snow ploughs 17
spacecraft 7, 29
Spruce Goose 23

tractors 8–9, 26
trains 21, 24, 26–27
trucks 4, 6–7, 9, 11, 12, 17, 24, 27, 28
tunnel-boring machines (TBMs) 20–21

wagons 13, 26
wheel loaders 11
wheels 4, 6, 8, 10, 12, 26, 27, 28
wings 23, 29